The Treasure Is Within You

Mimi Novic

Aspiring Hope
Publishing

British Library Cataloguing Publication Data.

A Catalogue record for this book is available from the British Library.

ISBN 978-1-9999120-9-3

Published by Aspiring Hope Publishing

Raising funds to support
The Prince's Trust

Prince's Trust

All net proceeds donated to The Prince's Trust.
A registered charity, incorporated by Royal Charter, in England and Wales (1079675) and Scotland (SC041198).

Dedication

In The Name Of God The Most Beneficent The Most Merciful & All Loving

For My Lala,

With my heartfelt Love and Gratitude for being the wind beneath my wings.
All My Love

For My SN

My Love encompasses eternity
All My Love

About Mimi Novic

Mimi Novic is one of today's bestselling inspirational authors and is ranked amongst the top names in inspirational, motivational and spiritual books in the world. Her writings and quotes are considered some of the most popular in modern times and are used by some of today's most well known and influential figures.

She is internationally known as one of the most respected and highly regarded motivational and self awareness teachers in the fields of self-development and spiritual growth. Her expertise has made her amongst the most popular and highly demanded well being experts of today.

Working as a complementary medical practitioner, self development teacher, voiceover artist, author and motivational speaker, Mimi has collaborated with some of the most well-known and knowledgeable therapists, composers, musicians, coaches, healers and professionals in their field and bringing together powerful teams that work in synchronicity to bring the best possible life enhancing experiences.

She teaches and runs workshops and seminars in a wide array of therapies, complementary medicine and self-awareness, working around the world in clinics, retreats and on a one to one basis.

For more information about Mimi Novic please visit:: www.miminovic.co.uk

Foreword

Welcome to The Treasure Is Within You.

Words have an immeasurable power to change our life, shaping our innermost being, penetrating the very essence of our spirituality and daily existence.

They hold the capacity to uplift, inspire, and heal, igniting the illumination of hope and fortitude within us.

Words are often referred to as swords of our conscience that can wound, divide, and sow seeds of strife, leaving scars and pain that linger long after they are spoken. They can also illuminate reach person we come into contact with, serving as beacons of light in the darkest of times, and knowing this magnitude of power that we hold within ourselves has far reaching consequences.

As we go through our daily lives, the words we choose to utter, can either build bridges towards each other, or put up the barriers of misunderstanding. Depending on our intention the tone and content of what we say determines whether we connect in harmony with someone or we sever the ties of tolerance.

They serve as the vessels through which intentions, beliefs, and emotions are expressed, influencing our perceptions of ourselves, others, and the world around us. Thus, it is paramount to speak with care, being mindful holding compassion at the forefront and realising that their utterances have a profound impact on our spiritual and physical journey and the collective human oneness.

Within this book you'll discover the transformative power of positive affirmations, which are designed to uplift your spirit, ignite your inner strength and guide you towards a life filled with joy, gratitude and abundance.

Affirmations are more than just words; they are manifestations of empowerment, that have the ability to help you reshape your thoughts and enable you to awaken your aspirations and lead a more meaningful life.

By choosing to affirm the positive aspects of your life, you invite a wave of positivity into every aspect of your being.

By using affirmations in your daily life, it offers a multitude of benefits that are far reaching and can significantly boost self esteem and confidence.

When you regularly affirm your worth, ability and capabilities, you start to believe in them more deeply. This heightened self belief translates into being more assertive and enables a greater willingness to take on challenges and conquer them.

Firstly, they act as a powerful antidote to negative self-talk, replacing doubt and fear with confidence, love and self love.

They also serve as anchors, grounding you in the present moment and reminding you of your magnificent worthiness and potential.

The present moment holds an unimaginable strength that if used wisely can transform the entire direction of our life.

Foreword

Positive words can act as a powerful tool in combating depression, anxiety, and other mental health issues. By focusing on affirming statements, individuals can break the cycle of negative thought patterns that contribute to these conditions, allowing room for a more positive and stable mental state.

Life is filled with ups and downs but what is important is that we build a resilience to all that happens to us. Moreover, incorporating affirmations into your daily routine allows you to retrain your mindset to one of steadfastness.

Affirmations align your thoughts with your deep aspirations and goals by keeping you focused and motivated.
By consistently affirming and repeating your intentions, you reinforce your commitment to your aims and objectives which increases your persistence to fulfil them.

We cannot ever guarantee anything in this world and daily stresses are an inevitable part of life, but how we deal with it makes all the difference. Affirmations can serve as a quick and effective stress relief aid, helping to centre your mind and calm your thoughts. Repeating calming and empowering statements can reduce stress levels and promote a sense of inner peace and tranquility.

Ultimately, the journey of affirmations is one of discovery and empowerment.
As you embark on this path of self awareness you have the limitless potential that resides within you.
Take the first steps to pursue the life you have always dreamed of. Go fearlessly in the pursuit of your dreams.
May everywhere you go be blessed with Love & Peace!

Mimi Novic

Imagine if we had the courage to say all those unspoken words that come to our lips,
Explored every feeling that made us feel alive,
How differently we would live.

Mimi Novic

Sometimes we can only find our true
direction when we let the wind of change
carry us.

Mimi Novic

Hope

When hope fills my heart,
I am guided towards a brighter day and hopeful
about all I do.

Trust

I trust in my life journey.
Every day I am confident knowing that there is
a light upon my path and it helps me through
every uncertainty I may encounter.

Beacon

I am a beacon of light that is inspiring others
with my firm belief in goodness.

Strength

My heart is my compass as I navigate life's hurdles with resilience and strength.

Embrace

As I embrace the beauty around me, it helps me
see my own radiance.
Which is a powerful force for positive change in
my life and the world around me.

Accept

As I accept myself,
Everything becomes clear knowing that this
moment is the dawn of new possibilities.

Wishes

Hope ignites my wishes and empowers me to
pursue them with courage.

Positive

I welcome positive experiences into my life with open arms,
Allowing them to help me become more fulfilled.

Faith

With faith as my constant companion,
I walk confidently towards the realisations of my
deepest dreams and aspirations.

Stronger

I am stronger than all my setbacks and fears.
I face each one of them with determination and
strength.

Freedom

I release everything that is holding me back and embrace the freedom that comes with my personal courage.

Guide

I trust in my inner guide to overcome any challenge that arises, knowing that nothing has any power over me.

Lasting

Each step I take towards conquering my
insecurities and fears,
Fills me with lasting confidence.

Worthy

I am worthy of living a life which is free from the constraints of anxiety and fear and I walk towards that freedom.

Choice

I make the choice to focus on all the bright possibilities in my life rather than the limitations.

Winner

With each day I am a winner, as I overcome obstacles and I grow stronger and more resilient.

Destiny

I am the master of my thoughts.
There is no one who can alter the course of my destiny apart from God.
I tread fearlessly towards all that is written for me with abundance.

Way

I welcome the power of my inner strength and courageously face any challenge that comes my way.

New

The belief in myself makes me feel blessed and allows me to step outside of my worries by enabling me to try new opportunities.

Grace

I trust in my ability to be able to handle whatever life brings me with grace.

soul

Every obstacle I overcome strengthens my
worthiness and fortifies my soul.

Bold

I am bold and fearless.
I choose to make bravery my friend knowing
that success lies on the other side of fear.

Shine

I am not defined by other people's opinions of
me.
Who I am is defined by my perseverance to be
my true self,
Trusting my heart to shine through.

Power

Whenever I am faced with uncertainty,
There is an unwavering daring of confidence
within me that helps me to navigate the
unknown with trust in a greater power.

Reason

With each step I take in the direction of
pursuing my true calling.
I am reminded that I am protected at all times
and nothing ever happens without a reason.

Wisdom

I am a warrior of peace.
My soul shines brightly in the face of all
darkness.
My inner wisdom guides me towards the light.

Giving

I am worthy of giving and receiving unconditional compassion to myself and all living beings and embracing its transformative power.

Empathy

The guiding force in my life is love.
It leads me to empathy and kindness that helps
me to understand my own heart and that of
others.

Nurture

By opening my heart abundantly to all that I am,
I am bringing fulfilling moments and
relationships into my life, that nurture me in
wonderful ways.

Divine

Every single act of kindness I show to myself
and those around me,
Is a reflection of the Divine grace that resides
within me.

Loving

I cherish my soul and love it infinitely.
This helps me to be more genuine and loving.

Respect

When I respect myself,
I can appreciate the deep connections this
brings with everyone I come into contact with.

Heals

Love heals all wounds and restores harmony to
all parts of my mind, body and spirit.
When I accept that I am a vessel of love,
Everything I do becomes an act of generosity.

Honour

I honour all that I am and celebrate my
magnificent uniqueness.
I accept everyone I meet as a manifestation of
beauty in their own splendid form.

Essence

The essence of my being is free to love whoever it wants.
It embraces the world with open arms extending the pureness of my sincerity beyond all boundaries.

Star

There is a guiding star within me encouraging me to live authentically and with kindness towards myself and others.

I Believe

I truly believe in all that I am and I trust myself
fully to achieve all of my goals.
As I welcome a strong belief in the strength that
resides inside me,
Self doubt fades away and can no longer have
any effect on me.

Road

My self belief is indestructible and my
confidence is unshakeable.
I am always ready and welcome a new direction
along the road towards my aspirations.

Heart

I trust fully in my intuition and have faith in
every step I take along the path that I'm walking
on.
There is no greater power than following your
heart.

Encounter

Every setback I encounter is an opportunity to learn something new about myself and to strengthen my belief in my capabilities.

Deserve

I deserve respect and love and all the blessings
that flow upon my life show me that I am being
looked after by a heavenly force.

Truth

I release all false beliefs that others have and embrace the the truth of boundless potential that lies within me.

Purpose

I trust in the wisdom of my life journey as it
unfolds,
As I know that everything that happens serves
my higher purpose.

Leah

The trust I have in my own heart is the
foundation of all my relationships.
It allows me to take bold leaps of faith towards
my ultimate peace.

Favour

Everything conspires in my favour when I become fearless and I trust in Divine guidance to lead me towards infinite possibilities.

Enrich

I always follow my intuition,
Allowing it to guide me towards the right
decisions and paths that enrich my journey.

Moving

When I practice the power of forgiveness,
I am able to release past hurts and accept the
freedom that comes with letting go and moving
on.

Timing

I am certain that there is a universal timing to
everything that happens.
This certainty allows me to be patient and
peaceful, knowing that everything which
unfolds has a Divine order.

Miracles

I trust in the power of God to move mountains
and manifest miracles in my life.

Enhance

When I let go of worry and doubt,
I surrender to the flow of serenity and
tranquility,
Knowing that every experience whether happy
or challenging, is a gift from above helping me
to enhance my soul.

Luminous

Within me radiates a luminous light that blesses
every aspect of my life.

Harmony

Calm is my natural state of being and I align
with all things that instill in me harmony.

Balance

I am an instrument of peace.
I spread calm and serenity wherever I go.
In the midst of conflicts, I remain centred and grounded,
Restoring balance and clarity.

Release

I gently release what no longer serves me,
Allowing me to create a space for new
beginnings and trust in the adventure of freeing
myself from the past.

Breath

I am free with each breath to explore new horizons and release all limitations and embrace the boundless possibilities of freedom.

Path

Every step I take I celebrate my freedom to walk my own path free of fear and doubt.

Liberate

I liberate myself from past mistakes and the
chains of negativity.
I am limitless and I find endless opportunities
while living positively.

Potential

I believe in my potential, knowing that all that is meant for me is within my reach.

Connect

I am connected to the Divine essence within
and around me,
Guiding my spiritual journey.

Sacred

Each moment is a sacred opportunity for me to embody enlightenment on my spiritual path.

Thread

I embrace the interconnectedness of all beings,
seeing how the Divine spark within each of us
joins everything with the thread of love.

Unity

In the stillness and calm,
I find my spirit recognising the unity of all
things.
Allowing me the space to honour all of creation.

Humble

I honour the differences in all people and accept them as an opportunity to teach me more about who I am and to help me be more humble.

Quest

In the quest for truth I am open minded and open hearted.
I transcend all prejudices and flaws about myself and let others be who they truly are without judgement.

Protect

With gratitude and humility,
I remind myself that I am allowed to set
boundaries in order to prioritise my needs and
protect my peace of mind.

Deserving

Every part of me is deserving of love,
Including the parts that I don't understand yet.
I treat myself with compassion and kindness,
Realising that I am a beautiful masterpiece.

Happiness

The source of my happiness is internal and strong.
It remains uniquely mine.
I peacefully let go of worries and embrace the present moment with deep gratitude.

Pleasures

I always try and find the simple pleasures and
beauty of everyday life.

Look

I trust that genuine joy is always within my
reach, no matter what the circumstances.
It all depends on how I look at things,
I choose to look with the eyes of love.

Journey

I eagerly reach out to everything that leads me
on an adventurous journey.

Start

Each day is a fresh start,
Full of new opportunities and possibilities.

Open

I release what upset me in the past and welcome the promise of new beginnings with an open heart.

Doorway

Every ending is an open doorway to a new
chapter in my life.

Begin

I forgive myself for all my mistakes and I am
open for the opportunity to begin again.

Pursuit

I am ready to step into the unknown with
courage and determination.
I let no one hold me back in the pursuit of my
hopes.

survive

With every fresh start, I uncover more about myself and my capabilities and I take pride in overcoming all that I've endured and all that I've survived.

Deserve

I let go of fear and doubt,
With the knowledge that new beginnings bring
endless possibilities for me and I deserve to be
given new chances.

Authentic

I embrace visibility, revealing my authentic self
to the world without hesitation.

Good

I am good enough.
I deserve a life that is incredible.

Spark

The radiance from within me cannot be dimmed
by anything outside of me.
My inner spark is eternal and solely mine.

Unique

I have been bestowed unique gifts that are
exclusively mine.
There is only one of me on this entire planet.

Moment

Every single day, I am edging nearer to reaching my goals.
With the might of my thoughts and words, remarkable changes are unfolding within me and in my life at this moment.

Message

My life speaks volumes to the world, Embodying the message of authenticity, purpose and compassion.

Conquer

I've triumphed over tough times and adversity before, emerging with greater strength and wisdom.
I am resilient and I am capable of conquering any challenge.

Value

I seize every moment of my life, extracting its
full worth every single day.
Today, tomorrow and every day thereafter, I
maximise the value of my time on this planet.

Progress

I refrain from comparing myself to others.
Instead, I measure my progress against my own
past self.
As long as I continue to improve even slightly
each day, I consider myself successful by my
own standards.
With each new beginning, I am reborn with a
newly found strength.

Knowing

I step into the unknown with a firm confidence
in myself,
Knowing that each new start holds the promise
of endless options for a better life.

Dawn

A single positive thought at dawn has the
potential to transform my entire day.
Today, I awaken with a positive intention,
shaping the tone of my day and inviting success
to resonate through each moment ahead.

Precisely

I am precisely where I need to be, at the perfect moment, engaged in the correct actions.

Decisions

I take responsibility for myself,
Beginning with my own actions and decisions.

Love

I deserve love simply for being myself.
Love is inherent to every individual, including
myself.
I am sufficient as I am.

Goodness

I deserve happiness and vitality in my life.
I am an integral part of this place.
My kindness uplifts others, fostering a
wonderful feeling within me.
I trust in my inherent goodness.

Victorious

I am stronger than I realise.
I've faced challenges before and emerged
victorious and I will do so again.
I am capable of overcoming difficult situations.

Worthy

I affirm my worthiness to pursue my desires
with confidence.
I assert control over my life and its direction.
I am exerting my utmost effort and recognising
that it is sufficient.

Celebrate

I express gratitude for the gift of life each day.
Today and every day, I am filled with blessings.
I embrace optimism, as each day presents a new
opportunity.
I anticipate a wonderful day ahead.
Today is a reason for celebration.
I am determined to achieve success.

Aware

I am aware of my value.
I nurture myself with kindness and compassion.
I grant myself the freedom to embrace my true self.
I harbour deep love for myself.
I have complete trust in myself.

Needs

I permit myself to prioritise my self care.
I deserve respect and kindness at all times.
My needs and wishes matter.
I have every right to feel good.

Nourish

Each day, I grow healthier and stronger.
I prioritise both my mental and physical
wellness.
I listen to my body and trust its wisdom.
I express gratitude for my body and its daily
efforts to help me.

Feats

I have the power and the ability to make
positive life decisions.
My body is capable of extraordinary feats.
I cherish my health as a precious gift.

Ease

I let go of concerns beyond my control.
Consistency brings ease and familiarity.
I have the strength to overcome anything.
I've overcome challenges before; I can do it
again.
I breathe in tranquility and release uncertainty.

Fresh

I choose how to deal with each day as it comes.
Tomorrow offers a fresh start and new
perspective.
A difficult day does not define my entire life.
I am not defined by my worries,
I have the choice to decide my daily
accomplishments.

Merit

I am present to offer my unique gifts to the world.
I refrain from criticising myself.
My voice holds significance.
I am deserving of the compliments I receive.
I merit all the goodness that comes my way.

Circle

I cultivate a circle of uplifting individuals who
inspire me.
I have the power to decide who enters my life.
I am complete on my own.
I do not depend on others for my happiness.
I am capable of releasing relationships that no
longer align with me.

Dignity

I affirm my worth and refuse to tolerate
disrespect from others.
I stand firm in asserting boundaries and demand
to be treated with dignity and respect.

Fearless

I welcome the courage within me to fearlessly
stand up for my beliefs,
Knowing that my voice has power and my
convictions are worthy of expression.

Entrust

I entrust every aspect of my life to the guidance
and care of God,
Trusting that His wisdom and love will lead me
through every situation with grace and strength.

www.ingramcontent.com/pod-product-compliance
Lightning Source LLC
Chambersburg PA
CBHW040936030426
42335CB00001B/11